Kim Ki Duk

On Movies, the Visual Language

Kim Ki Duk

On Movies, the Visual Language

Marta Merajver-Kurlat

Jorge Pinto Books Inc.
New York

Published by Jorge Pinto Books Inc., website: www.pintobooks.com

Cover design © 2009 by Nigel Holmes, website: www.nigelholmes.com

Back cover photography by Mi-Ok Kim

Book design by Charles King, website: www.ckmm.com

ISBN 978-1-934978-17-7
    1-934978-17-5

WORKING BIOGRAPHY SERIES

Contents

흰색과 검은색은 같은 색이다

감기덕

Kim Ki DUK

(White and black are the same color.)

Acknowledgments

I wish to thank all the wonderful people without whose help this biography could not have been written.

First of all, publisher Jorge Pinto, who engineered and facilitated this project with his proverbial enthusiasm and constant encouragement. It goes without saying that I am deeply grateful to filmmaker Kim Ki Duk for providing the background material on which I drew to develop the book. His generous, extensive answers to my questions enabled me to grasp the essence of his work and professional choices while giving me an insight into most valuable, alternative ways of approaching the making of a film.

Last but not least, Jerome Lee and Sabina Lee, both with Book Seventeen Agency, were instrumental to the process of putting together the pieces of this rather unusual writing technique as described in the Introduction. My special thanks to them; for I would have found myself at a dead end had it not been for their cooperation.

Foreword

Writing this biography has been a unique experience. I am specifically thinking of the mode that the work adopted, since my subject, director-laureate Kim Ki Duk, lives literally at the other end of the world. We have never met. We have not even corresponded, for he speaks, reads, and writes Korean only (although I suspect this is not exactly so, he adamantly insists on it) and I do not know a single word of his language.

The "interviews," if one may call them so, consisted of questions that I sent, in English, to my publisher, who relayed them to Mr. Kim's interpreter. The interpreter translated the questions into Korean, made a note of the answers or received them in writing from Mr. Kim, translated them into English, and they made their way back to me through my publisher. When quoting from this source, I have transcribed the sentences verbatim, for fear that a cultural bias on my part might affect the intended meaning or misrepresent Kim to the reader. My decision not to make any changes was further supported by the Korean translator, who wrote that the "translation is done to follow his [Kim's] choice of words and style as closely as possible."

Some of the material that I received resembled the free association technique, for which I am extremely grateful, since it provided me with much more than I had dared to ask. On the other hand, Mr. Kim strongly believes that it is not up to him to explicate his work, so I was left with much less than I hoped for regarding his movies. Since many artists in different fields feel that the truth, rather than beauty, "is in the eyes of the beholder," I expect the reader to seek for his/her own comprehension of Kim's works inside their own hearts.

You do not need to think; this is not an intellectual exercise. You need to watch, to watch carefully, and to open all your senses to what is on the screen. You will probably discover that, at some point or other, you too were there.

"There" is not a physical place. It is a moment in life, suspended in mid-air; it is a sensation you cannot describe; it is a tear, a smile, a shiver. Something coming from a place with no name will pierce into some equally nameless part of you. And your emotions will flow into the river that connects the past with the future, the real with the imaginary, the doable with the impossible.

If you have already seen Kim's movies, you know what I am talking about. If you have not, it is time to peek into the amazing world of one of the most remarkable film makers of our times.

M.M.K.

Kim Ki Duk

With its unprecedented growth for such a small country in a relatively short period of time, we tend to view South Korea as a kaleidoscope of state-of-the art electronic gadgets, a modern, puissant state, and a place where serendipity is taken for granted.

We are not mistaken. Still, such achievements weigh heavily on a working class that keeps rolling the wheels of progress without enjoying many of its benefits.

It is striking that in this time, as in others before, one individual should rise above his class, his life circumstances, the toils he seemed to be destined to, to stand out as a great creator, one who is saluted as such by the globalized world. A creator who, after coming into direct contact with European culture, decided to return to his homeland and depict the world at large. We may be deceived into believing that Kim Ki Duk's movies are about the differences between East and West, Korean people, and their predicaments. He himself will tell us that he is concerned with something else, and that nationality is not an issue in his stories.

Kim Ki Duk is a living example that when there is a will there is a way. Born in Bonghwa, North Gyeongsang Province, in 1960, he and his family moved to Seoul in his early childhood. The horizon ahead seemed to offer the monotonous pattern of a working class life. His choices lay between becoming a farm laborer or a blue-collar worker. His family neither expected nor encouraged the boy to choose differently. However, the unexpected spark of art ran deep in him. He dutifully undertook to fulfill the family mandate, first by trying agricultural school, and then by taking a job in a factory. Perhaps the time he devoted as a volunteer to aid the blind strengthened his desire to make those who had been blessed with sight to actually see; to raise awareness of the self and of others by using not only their eyes, but the eyes of all dormant senses.

Speaking about his adolescence, this acclaimed director says that, until age 30, when he spent every coin he had been able to scrape on a one-way ticket to Paris, he never had a respite from manual or automated jobs, depending on the circumstances, going from an auto junkyard to a button factory to an electronics manufacturing company to construction sites. As we will see later, he does not in the least regret these experiences. But it is unavoidable to feel the poignancy of the phrase "*I lived always tired.*"

Unlike people with the possibility of finding answers in an exchange with either peers or books, Kim Ki Duk posed himself questions whose answers he needed to find for himself. He wanted to know why humans had to endure such physical and emotional hardship. That an uncultivated mind—as his was then—wondered about human fate in these terms is, to say the least, surprising. But that he tried to reach some explanation by writing scenarios is certainly amazing.

His lifelong hobby (painting), which demands a special capacity of observation and the ability to see beyond the surface of things, may have stood him in good stead when he made up his mind to take a step forward into the moving image. The leap was prompted by the first three films he saw in his life: *The Silence of the Lambs*, *Les amants du Pont Neuf*, and *The Lover*, based on Marguerite Duras's novel. This and the Parisian atmosphere, perhaps, since Kim had never stepped into a movie theater before his arrival in Paris.

A superficial view might suggest that this is yet another version of the rags-to-riches story. Far from it, this director's success is a direct consequence of his determination to keep true to himself, regardless of the outcome. This is one case in which it is impossible to draw a line between personal feelings and choice of career.

The following pages intend to show that it is not necessary to forego one's inner quest and sheepishly adapt to the ways of the world for the sake of recognition. In other words, the message is that self-betrayal may produce an imitation of art, but true art stems from a true heart.

New Beginnings

It might not be easy for the Western mind to figure out why a thirty-year old man living in a crowded, busy city like Seoul never watched a movie. Perhaps it would help to briefly review the history of Korean cinema so as to understand the ways of the industry.

According to Professor Cho Hee-Moon*, public screenings in Korea started in a most unusual way. Henry Collbran, whom the government had commissioned to electrify Seoul, offered the local workers performances in an attempt to motivate them to work faster. These performances were so welcome that Collbran wasted no time in expanding his construction business and adding an entertainment department to his company.

Public screenings of Western movies enthralled the Korean public, as they felt that what they saw on screen reflected a way of life totally different from theirs, and that watching these movies bridged the wide gap between two cultures that had little if anything in common.

However, the educated class and the general public did not see eye to eye on the matter. While the former encouraged movie going in the belief that proximity with and learning from the West were enriching and profitable, the latter regarded films as cheap entertainment,

---

* http://www.labobe.edu.au/screeningthepast/reruns/rr1298/CBrr5a.html, last visited January 2009.

and failed to apprehend the educational aspects of the novelty.

The first cinema, an open-air one, seems to have opened as early as 1903, and soon a number of movie-theaters favored the trend. The cinemas were well attended in daily screenings. All seemed to go well until the Japanese annexation in 1910. Although the Japanese occupation did not discourage filmmaking, film production was subject to heavy censorship. Other countries, like France and the United States, were granted permission to shoot films in Korea, often about local themes. Foreign producers and crews then took their products to be exhibited elsewhere; thus, the Japanese did not worry that this could pose a threat on their rule. What they did realize was that this form of entertainment could also be a powerful vehicle for propaganda, which could work for or against colonial interests. Then the Japanese kept a close watch on items that might encourage patriotic, potentially revolutionary feelings, while they themselves made and exhibited movies that fostered expected behaviors (health care, saving habits, fire prevention, etc.).

The Koreans were not explicitly banned from making films. In fact, a number of movies, mostly documentaries, were shot and duly lost in the long years that ended with the Japanese withdrawal from the territory in 1945 in the aftermath of their defeat by the Allies in World War II. Still, the country had to engage in yet another war (1950–1953) after the split in which South Korea remained independent from foreign rule but was invaded by Soviet- and China-driven North Korea.

Although South Korea did not fall prey to its Communist neighbors, the war took a heavy toll on the country. It is indeed a miracle that, despite time spent at reconstruction, with dictatorial governments raising their heads now and then, Korea has grown into the Asian Tiger whose technological developments and distinct culture are closely watched and followed by the West.

The Calling

The film industry was not left behind in Korea's gigantic growth, a fact which still leaves us with the question "Why did Kim Ki Duk not watch a movie in his own country?" buzzing in our ears. In an interview conducted by film critic Kim So-Hee,* the director declared that "production by manual labor is the only worthwhile thing in life. Culture is a mere luxury." However, when I asked him this very question in December 2008, the answer was radically different. Kim said, and I quote:

> *Working at factories since the age of 15, I lived a life far from having cultural activities and thought movies were unattainable fantasies for people like me. I had always thought that film was a type of culture that could be appreciated only by those who are college graduates. People like me who were factory workers wouldn't be able to understand such a level of sophisticated culture. I think that, before arriving in Paris, I thought movies were meaningless entertainment. At any rate, to me the film world was too distant, far away, and a different realm of reality at that time. I couldn't even fathom thinking about watching one.*

---

* http://www.cinekorea.com/filmmakers/kimkiduk.html, last visited January 2009.

The answer given to the critic suggests a black-and-white view of reality based on a deeply rooted ideology. On the other hand, the explanation offered in 2008 shows maturity, reflection, and inner search. It also sheds light on what many blue-collar workers must have felt about a world divided between "them" and "us," a world in which "sophisticated culture" (theirs) lay at the other side of an unfathomable ocean into which "we" were bound to drown if "we" ever attempted to swim across.

The choice of Paris also arouses a number of questions. While it is true that in the late 1950s through the 1960s France had taken the lead in changing the rules of the cinematic game, other countries, notably Italy and England, were also pioneering novel uses of the camera. In fact, had Italian neorealism not preceded the French *nouvelle vague*, the French innovators of the time might well have taken a different course.

Be it as it may, Kim Ki Duk arrived in Paris with literally nothing in his pockets. He scraped a living as a street painter, and no doubt wandered around the City of Light, awed at the layout, the architecture, and the people.

At some point, his feet dragged him into a movie theater. Kim confesses to having been deeply struck by three films that let him *"have certain dreams about films and movie-making."*

The Silence of the Lambs and *Les amants du Pont Neuf,* the first two films he mentions, were both shot in 1991, while *The Lover* is a 1992 production. He must have watched a number of others, but his insistence on how these films somehow thrust him into doing something else with his life surely deserves special attention. Perhaps it is worth going over these films to get a glimpse of what may have inspired his dreams.

The Silence of the Lambs, based on a novel by Thomas Harris, is a psychological, hair-raising thriller featuring Anthony Hopkins and Jodie Foster. Hannibal Lecter (Hopkins), an anthropophagous serial killer serving a life sentence, guides young FBI cadet Clarice Starling (Foster) along the path that will enable her to catch another serial killer who flays his victims. The striking thing about this strange association is that Lecter, whose (presumably) second occupation was psychiatry, exercises his professional skills in a psychiatrist-patient mimic of a real treatment, with Starling contributing all the defense mechanisms and denial that a real patient would. By the end of the film, success in bringing the killer to justice is much less important than the healing process undergone by Starling. Much as she tries to shun Lecter's interventions on her repressed experiences, his ability to utter the right remarks at the moments when she is most vulnerable or most receptive sweeps away such fears as she would not admit to herself. For a better understanding of Kim's approach to man's predicament, perhaps it would be useful to clear up what is usually understood by "repressed experiences." There is a general belief that our unconscious is some sort of pit that needs digging into, sometimes for years on end, to access the cause of our uneasiness. This belief does not take into account Freud's theory of the return of the repressed.

Quite simply, if we just listen to the phrase without getting lost into the maze of psychoanalytical theory, this means that it is not necessary to "dig" in order to find the causes of our anxiety. These causes resurface time and again in the formations of the unconscious (dreams, slips, jokes, and parapraxes in general). Their repetition, adopting different forms at different times, *is* the repressed. Thus, the outer story (the chase of a murderer) becomes only a pretext to deploy the innermost recesses of an anguished mind and the concomitant ability of the psychiatrist-murderer to isolate the return of the repressed and lift the repression. One might venture to say that this movie may have shown Kim that the darkest, unspeakable aspects of a "normal" human being can be found in every one of us, regardless of the face we show to the world. Incidentally, Kim does not speak of psychoanalytic theories, though philosophical and metaphysical concerns prompt most of his scenarios. Still, when he tells us, as you will see, that his films are about conscience, one cannot but think that the unconscious (what we are not aware that we know) is, borrowing from Disraeli, "conspicuous by its absence."

Leos Carax's *Les amants du Pont Neuf* (released in English-speaking countries under the title *The Lovers on the Bridge*), is basically a love story. Some may wonder what can be particularly striking about the subject matter, since love stories probably account for an impressive percentage of the film history in all countries. But here, precisely, lies the rub. Most love stories are spiced with one or more of the following ingredients: eroticism, sex, jealousy, hesitation, repentance, threats from the outside world, or what you will. Although this film includes characters other than the two protagonists—Michèle, a painter who made her home in the streets because of an ill-starred romantic relationship crowned by a disease that would eventually lead to blindness, and Alex, a street performer suffering from serious addictions—what really matters is naked love. If anything, the squalor of their lives, the way in which they slowly learn about each other's miseries draws them closer. Neither of them can stand the mere thought of losing the other. Stripped of its trappings, love tends to appear as a disposable trinket. Not in this film, though, in which love is depicted in a most unconventional form for the times. This love is not extolled, sung, or presented as the epitome of a noble feeling. Rather, it just happens and, according to the movie, needs no justification. Perhaps *The Lovers on the Bridge* prompted in Kim the desire to explore the mysteries of love, of the substance we are made of.

The Lover, based on Marguerite Duras's novel *L'amant*, also plumbs the depths of one way in which we humans approach love. Shot in 1992 by Jean-Jacques Arnaud, the story picks up the thread of Duras's obsession, which could be aptly expressed by James Carver's title *What We Talk About When We Talk About Love**. In fact, in 1958 the then 26-year old near-beginner Louis Malle had made another of her novels, *Les amants* [*The Lovers*],

---

* Carver, Raymond. *What We Talk About When We Talk About Love*; The Harvill Press, London, Panther Edition, 1993.

into a film. Interestingly enough, actress Jeanne Moureau, the lead of this film, lent her voice to *The Lover* as the unseen narrator who fills in the information aesthetically removed from dialog and image.

Set in Vietnam some ten years after the end of World War I, this film/novel—the terms are interchangeable here, since the director respected the text in a most laudable way—is a pageant of opposites, of what cannot be, of what shocks the true-blue bourgeois of all epochs. At that time of life when our hormones run amok to the extent that we catch fevers that cannot be accounted for, a white French adolescent whose family has come down in life stuns a wealthy, supposedly experienced Chinese upper-class young man. He is devoured by desire, and plays all the tricks that money and privilege can buy in order to have her. "Have" is not an exaggeration. In fact, he wants to possess her, to own her, to be her master and her slave. And then hell breaks loose. It would be unfair to say that he loves her straightaway, at this moment when he is ready to pounce on her as if he were hunting a rare specimen. During their encounters, she has the advantage over him, for her discovery of sexuality does not yield to her greed. She wants to explore sensuality without forgetting for a second that he is so trapped in their relationship that she can ask for the moon and the stars (read this as plenty of money and money substitutes). Finally, arousal engenders love; love sets their sweating bodies on fire; their thirst for each other is never quenched. Love, as conveyed on the screen, is sour-sweet, endless joy, everlasting pain, brutal attraction, angry rejection, and so much more.

This particular relationship goes against all the rules: neither family would condone that their race be tainted by the "unclean" other. Besides, her mother would never get over the loss of her precious virginity out of wedlock, while many years ago his father had already arranged his marriage to a suitable match. Thus they part. He will love her forever. She, who has gone from curiosity to teasing to exploiting her power over him, discovers that she has loved him. From now on, she will love the shadow of her love.

Before making an educated guess about what may have struck Kim Ki Duk about this film, let me say a few words about language. When Kim spoke about these films, he named *Les amants du Pont Neuf* in French, which was the language spoken in the film, and *The Silence of the Lambs* in English. But he called Arnaud's film *The Lover*, even when he saw it in Paris. In a rather ambivalent way, Kim gives no importance to languages, understood as systems of communication. When asked how he had managed to get by in Paris without even a perfunctory knowledge of French, he answered,

> *[I learned] very little; I memorized nouns and verbs to live. At times, it was a blessing that I didn't understand the language, which was also a cause of frustration. However, I didn't want to learn and live with a deep knowledge of the [French/U.S.] society and history. I could know many things*

through the people's expressions and behavior. Even
now, I think that it is fortunate for me not to know
too much about English or European languages.

In other words, verbal language does not matter. If
you can decode other languages, those of bodies and
colors, for example, communication is achieved. So if
he must resort to verbal language, as was the case with
the preparations prior to the writing of this book, Kim
will reach out for what is handiest. We will take this up
further on, when we come to the issue of dialog in his
films.

Going back to the deep impression *The Lover* made
on him, perhaps it had to do with the fact that it deals
with universals. Feelings in the raw, feelings that anyone
can experience, regardless of age, race, and time. The
reader may wonder why he/she is not being offered Kim's
own reasons for the "before" and "after" that these films
meant to his life. The answer is simple. Having been told
that these three films *"were an inspirational shock,"* and
warned that his movies—and movies in general, probably—*"are not a roundtable table discussion,"* I refrained
from asking.

Away from Home

A number of articles about Kim Ki Duk place his artistic awakening in Paris. It is a good thing, then, that he lays emphasis on the fact that he liked painting before even thinking of traveling abroad. Though he spent time in the French capital, he visited

> *most of the art museums in Europe and saw many paintings, sculptures, and photos, all of which inspired me and my later film endeavors. Especially, I was more moved by sculptures on [random] streets and markings of the past than art works at museums. Particularly, sculptures in some nameless Hungarian village really made an impact.*

The reference to the sculptures triggers some reflections. Indeed, some of his films present magnificent shots of ancient and modern Korean sculptures. But the composition of a sculpture and the techniques required are sometimes intuited in takes of real people and everyday objects; living sculptures that are rearranged time and again, offering an unsuspected variety of aesthetic possibilities.

Judging from his narrative, it would seem that the "Paris myth" arose from the widespread belief that Paris and painting were one and the same thing. Kim is talking about what Koreans thought in those times, and he was no exception. In 1990, he says, *"I went there to paint."*

Kim's life in Paris was not restricted to painting, although he must have absorbed everything else through the eyes of a painter. Born painters may need some training in the use of their tools, but no "school-made" painter will acquire the special gaze that takes in at once what ordinary people miss. The painter sees beyond the surface of things and people, grasping the essence that is so often concealed by shape, color, clothing, or make-up. Just like anybody else who finds himself in the midst of an alien society, he was hit in the solar plexus by the cultural shock. Curiously enough, it first happened at the movie theater, where the only possible interaction is between the spectator's mind and senses and the action developing on the screen. There is no chance of sharing or contact, as *The Purple Rose of Cairo** so cleverly over-turned; still, the spectator can and often does speculate on and/or identify with what he is watching. Apparently, Kim had previous assumptions about the first film that he watched, and he discovered that the discourse he had so far sustained about films was not realistic. He says, *"The story of the film wasn't much different from what I had imagined, hence I became interested [in films]."*

The idea that making a film was nothing out of this world became strengthened by his observation of the French. They were utterly different from the people he knew in Korea. The insight that

---

* *The Purple Rose of Cairo*, 1985, directed by Woody Allen.

> *whether homeless or whomever [I encountered],*
> *I watched everyone there had their own sense of*
> *identity and embraced it in their life confidently*

operated a change in his vision of himself.

> *I became also confident in myself and in my*
> *abilities as I observed them and found myself*
> *wanting to write a scenario while watching mov-*
> *ies. Thereafter, I went back to Korea and started*
> *work in movies.*

One might wonder at the fact that a sojourn in a foreign country should have the force to change the course of a life. The decision to try an alternative way of conveying personal observation resulted in Kim eventually becoming an icon. He was not certainly aiming at that; it just happened, probably because he had something to say that the world needed to hear. However, if he had stuck to painting and had been fortunate enough to exhibit his works in museums, the scope of his audience would surely have been very limited. His message—the message he dares us to decode by ourselves—would have been sadly lost in the sound and the fury of contemporary art.

Back in Korea

In 1993, when he decided to return home, two things were crystal-clear to Kim. One was that he could get into the movie milieu by writing film scenarios, and the other that he definitely did not want to go back to a factory worker's life.

He took positive action by registering at a scenario writing workshop, but it took some time for him to tell his family and friends that he was planning to abandon the only way of life that all of them regarded as "natural." He says *"they were not the kind of folks who were in a position to give any assistance to my endeavors in film,"* and one can easily picture the situation, as it is duplicated in every working class family all over the world. In truth, it would be too much to ask of people whose sustenance had depended on labor for generations to acknowledge that something vaguely related to the arts was a wise choice.

Eventually, he had to open up to his family. They tried to discourage him in every possible way, and this too is understandable. They were in no position to support a 33-year old son while he trod a most slippery path which, in their view, would lead to nowhere, and they fretted about his future. If sayings such as "a bird in hand is worth two in the bush" exist in Korean, they must have drummed his ears at all times of day.

My family was against my screen-writing effort citing [lack of] living expenses [generated from it] and I often wrote on the streets with my typewriter while I was drawing portraits of passers-by. However, I felt very ashamed and embarrassed about painting on the streets. Always had a hat deeply pushed down on my head covering my head and wrote scenarios.

This shows the extent of Kim's determination to achieve his purpose or, at least, to give it a fair chance until he proved who was right. Embarrassment is a great deterrent. And yet it is quite extraordinary that somebody who has reached the top makes no bones about freely admitting that he felt ashamed. This goes to show that integrity is an asset in life as well as in art. When you sense the truth in a man's words, you believe that his art also conveys some truth for you to discover.

Those of his same social standing who wished him well were equally troubled by his "eccentricity." "*There were many times that people advised me saying even college graduates couldn't do what I was attempting to do . . . encouraging me to give up,*" he remembers. Others were much harder on him, and did not mince words: "If you, Kim Ki Duk, become a screen writer, I shall burn my own fingers."

Kim could not care less whether they burned just their fingers or their whole hand. He single-mindedly devoted his time and energy to the task in front of him, making the best of his experience at the writing workshop. He recalls that he was scared because all his classmates were university graduates, while he had finished only elementary school. Some of the others had majored in literature, yet his stories received much praise from the instructors. As he had not gone to university, he learned not only from his teachers but also from other students, particularly what he calls "scenario grammar." There was no wishful thinking or daydreaming at that time of his life. Since he was not making a living out of labor, he turned scenario writing into "labor" and *worked every day accordingly.* He finished one feature-length film every month, for he was perfectly aware that unless he became a professional writer soon so that his scripts could make the big screen, he would have to go back to factory work, an intolerable idea that sharpened his wits to give the best of himself.

Of the ten screen plays that he wrote that year, *A Painter and a Criminal Condemned to Death* won first prize from the Korean Educational Institute of Screenwriting, and within twelve months Kim made his debut as a director of his own film. With absolute candor, he remarks,

I ran into a lot of [operational] problems because I didn't study film or production. Therefore, I threw out films I shot early in my endeavor. In that time of struggle, I shot for four months and completed a film called Alligator, and even if the methods were far from perfection, it earned a favorable review as a meaningful film.

Such Stuff as Films Are Made On

Paraphrasing Shakespeare's* phrase—*"such stuff as dreams are made on"*—does not sound irrational, since Kim spoke about "having certain dreams about films and movie making" and his films exude, at least in the view of some audiences, a dream-like atmosphere. Perhaps it would not be a waste of time to bear in mind that not all dreams are pleasant, and that nightmares were also commanded by Queen Mab.

Alligator, more frequently known by the name of *Crocodile*, was released in 1996 and attracted the attention of critics and audiences alike. Crocodile is a homeless, extremely violent ruffian who lives under a bridge in Seoul with two other marginals. One day, a beautiful young woman who has suffered an amorous disappointment attempts suicide by jumping into the river from the bridge. Crocodile fishes her out and forces himself on her. She could have left had she wanted to, but for some reason she decided to stay and the four of them lived as a rather peculiar "family." Crocodile's inborn violence would not be tempered, and when he brought irreparable trouble upon himself, the young woman attempted suicide for the second time.

One image is worth a thousand words, so I have offered a very brief overview of the plot's shell only to

---

* Shakespeare, William. *The Tempest*, Act IV, Scene I.

introduce the effect it had on women. It cannot be denied that the tip of the iceberg sighted in the paragraph above reveals an almost intolerable amount of violence. It seems that many of the women who actually saw the movie failed to read the individual and social metaphors that were written all over it. Their eyes remained fixed on the brutality and degradation staring at them from the screen, and they called Kim a psycho among other unpalatable epithets.

These anti-Kim feelings became even more deeply rooted as his next movies were released, to the extent that some feminist movements embraced campaigns against them as if they feared these movies might further imperil women's lives in countries with serious gender problems.

When asked about this attitude, Kim took it calmly.

Female critics labeled it [Crocodile] as a "rape" film, and even now there are people who consider my films as anti-feminist and derogatory to females in general.

Kim's reaction to these attacks is very far from that of a bull to a red flag. Having pondered over the matter, he makes very clear distinctions into the various groups of women and their predicaments:

There are many diverse feminists, ranging from just a female to a female activist to a female college. When it is a group, some movies become their flag or, in my films' case, it becomes their political target. There are times when only a cut from my movies is required for their ideology, but if you watch my entire film, you may consider me to be a feminist. Therefore, I think there are various possible interpretations. Whether they use my films to be a model of female derogation or a weapon, all in each case is their problem. If they find my movies unpleasant, that's because they only think of the feminist movement without knowing life as a whole. I make movies about people rather than movies about women.

"Feminism" can be read as a portmanteau word that enwraps stances at odds with one another. When radical feminists wield the flag of gender rights, they tend to think in terms of one gender only (their own), systematically trashing men and feeling violated if men speak about women "as though they knew." Life as a whole entails very complex interactions between persons of the same gender and persons of both genders, and there is no doubt that these interactions are present in Kim's films in their full complexity. That, in his own words, he himself may sometimes be regarded as a feminist is evidenced by his deep comprehension of the diversity and the feelings that run deep below the cultural traits that our still patriarchal society has branded on women.

Apart from the many facets of life that his films delve into, the issue of women seems to be a constant preoccupation. It should be noted that his women are always shown inside a relationship with men, and that the darkest, most hidden, and hideous thoughts entertained by women come to light at some point. No doubt women who, in the different cultures, have been encouraged to fight their drives and set examples of endurance, understanding, and the endless list of "female differences/qualities" do resent being thus exposed.

Another item that these women do not seem to grasp is that love is often addressed at a male who does not precisely stand out for his unblemished character. Pascal's* phrase "The heart has reasons that reason cannot know" is not a sheer witticism. Love, one of the riddles that Kim turns this way and that in all his films, springs under the most unlikely circumstances. He makes no effort to explain it away; he just shows a range of events in which love rules over any other consideration. Thinking about critics and audiences, one might conclude that men, who are more given to impulse and action, will not question this, while women, the reflexive gender, cannot accept disclosure of their own nature, carefully covered by layer after layer of self-control.

Anyway, Kim remains unruffled at vicious attacks. In Korea more often than abroad, and with a few exceptions, women critics did their utmost to discredit him, while many male critics simply ignored him. He calmly states that he makes movies *"based on what he sees and feels,"* and that he does not read novels or books written by others.

---

* Blaise Pascal, French mathematician, physicist, and philosopher, 1623–1662.

Let us tackle the second statement first. To say the least, it is quite unusual for a creator to show no curiosity about what his fellow-writers are producing, if only to find out whether someone else is pursuing a line of thought similar to his. Nevertheless, this director's mind is so filled with his own questions that it would seem there is no room to even consider his colleagues' professional approach.

Living my life as such, I always asked about the irony I felt. Such questions are my movies, and if foreign critics find them interesting, that is because they also live their lives asking the same questions I am asking. My movies project questions.

This partly explains his indifference to the works of others. The notion of irony in this context is open to a number of interpretations, though from the content of his movies I am inclined to believe that it refers to the maladjustment between nature and nurture, between the primitive creatures that we are and the restrictions imposed on us by social convention, or between our random well-being and our equally random suffering. As to the questions, he does not expect answers from the outside. I think that his key is asking the right questions, the ones that are meaningful to him, and that the answers—supposing they exist—would detract from the significance of the questions. While some might think that the natural assumption about others living their lives asking the same questions gives away an egotistic, self-centered personality, a closer view might disclose that Kim merges with humanity in a single, universal quest.

I don't think that it is desirable to receive many questions about my movies. If it could just be felt, understood, and shared, there is no need for explanation.

Indeed, his movies project very uncomfortable questions about human nature, the life-death cycle, the contradictions inherent to the relationship between man and technology/science/progress and the like. He rejects the established forms in which art has been known to pose similar questions, and firmly upholds his opposition to be guided along much trodden paths:

I believe that expressions go beyond already determined lines of morality and ethics into a new territory. The world controls us with red and green lights [as in traffic lights]; expressions have rainbow colors, limitless shades.

Kim takes full advantage of these shades, but does not intend to gather a flock of followers or to rise as a prophet for change.

I do not want to become a philosopher or a powerful authority figure. [I want to] feel sad, angry . . . and try to understand about the world we live in and, in the process of it all, I want to eventually overcome. That's why I feel so pained, sad, and happy about making films and while I spend time making a film.

Prompted by the beauty of the composition in his movies, some of which strike the eye as a neat arrangement of a flawless series (*Spring, Summer, Autumn, Winter . . . and Spring*, for example), I asked him whether his earlier experience as a painter had influenced his present aesthetics, also remarkable for not relying heavily on dialog.

I did paint and photograph . . . and that, of course, was helpful in some part, but I think that movie making is about consciousness rather than what I did briefly in painting, music, or the experience in the mechanical/manufacturing environment. The people I met in my living through different spaces influenced my movies in a major way.

I do not intentionally reduce dialog [in my films]. Merely, I consider silence to be words [as well]. Silence is words in the most varied sense. And then I consider laughter and tears to be very brilliant dialog [next to silence]. Words coming out of a mouth have nuance . . . more than one meaning. Depending on the topic of a film, I think that meanings of dialogs always differ.

Consciousness of the self and of others should come to us as naturally as breathing, but is, in fact, difficult to achieve. Some people attend courses or seminars to catch just a glimpse of the meaning of consciousness, while others hope that by copycatting the "enlightened" they will gain the ability to exercise consciousness. There are also those who believe that it is enough to fix your eyes on something or somebody and to listen to words and sounds. What is being overlooked in this simplification is that endogenous and exogenous observation and listening need processing in order to acquire meaning.

Kim says that painting, music, and working in factories was helpful but not essential to his filmmaking. Yet all three activities demand constant observation of a setting, of the details, and of one's own movements and sensations. Even the most abstract styles of painting, often incomprehensible to the layman, presuppose an inner distribution of expressions in the invisible space of the mind. Keeping these imaginary "objects" in place without skipping the necessary steps involved in processing them until the work is finished would be impossible without the active intervention of consciousness. In other words, consciousness is a processing apparatus. The same can be said about labor. Let consciousness of your movements take a momentary break, and you may end losing a finger or worse. The trouble with focusing on what consciousness spells out for us all the time is that it leads to fatigue, insofar as it is interrelated with attention, and we know that after a time attention dwindles. To prevent us from fatal damages to our bodies and/or to our exchanges with others, we have been blessed with the capacity of "floating attention." This is a process during which, when nothing important is happening, the threshold of attention keeps at its lowest to reemerge with all its strength as soon as it is needed again.

What Kim tells us about dialog, words, silence, and other manners of conveying thoughts and feelings would fit into a great treatise about language, provided that grammarians, linguists, semiologists and other experts were broad-minded enough. Silent movies were self-explanatory, and when the spoken cinema (aptly called "the talkies") swept them away, there was something to win and something to lose. The human voice and its modulations reach sensitive areas of the seat of our emotions, and so do moans, sighs, sobs, and laughter. However, the mechanistic communication theory requires the use of a code (the spoken/written language) shared by both sender and receiver, for a message to be encoded by the former and decoded by the latter. Expressed thus, sounds that cannot be recognized as words are meaningless, and silence is a bottomless void into which the receiver can throw whatever meaning best suits his line of thought. Of course, this is just a poor, oversimplified description of the core of the theory. What I would like to stress in this respect is "no words = no communication." Discourse analysis brought considerable improvement to the field, and then other manners of language—e.g., body language, in which we could include silent tears—accounted for the numberless ways in which humans try to communicate.

Now, when Kim is wary of the nuances of words, he is actually touching a very soft spot. Words have denotations (only to be found in the factual aspects of language, in the established code, where the mental representation of a word will necessarily be the same for all those who share the code) and connotations, or extended meanings contained within metonymy and metaphor. Sometimes the context—not necessarily verbal, but situational—and the co-text help make the right connections, but there is no guarantee this will happen. From that point of view, provided that the combination of elements in a scene leads the viewer in the desired direction, the fewer words the better. Precisely because of their multiple meanings, of their connotations, words may mislead and distract.

On the other hand, the notion that silence amounts to words would drive diehard traditional linguists out of their minds, but it could not be truer. Silence does not suggest blankness. Rather, it draws attention to a thesaurus brimming with all the words available to the speaker of a language. It is up to the interlocutor to take his/her pick. You may argue that, supposing they share the same wavelength, communication will occur. You may further object that this is not frequent, especially when gender issues are at stake. Well, you would be right in saying so. But in Kim's films words tend to foster miscommunication or absence of communication. I am thinking of a particular scene in *Time*, in which the words spoken by a couple of lovers in bed ends up in tragedy, and it is only after a long, painful process of silence that they can finally communicate outside the boundaries of words.

This last sentence, for example, if read strictly in terms of the words that compose it, gives "communication" a positive connotation. But nothing could be further from the truth.

The issue of irony is recurrent in Kim's reflections. At one point, he says that he wants *"to proceed toward an area of overcoming those ironies [in the world I live in]."*

If reaching that realm involves killing someone (in a scenario) then I kill and forgiving, I did.

Indeed, the violence in some of his films is hardly bearable. Even if we agree that it is necessary for the development of the plot, we flinch in our seats. His film *Bad Guy* (2002) provides an example of extreme physical and psychological violence shown as the normal lifestyle in a world that most spectators have not experienced first hand. Before going over an interview in which Kim, against his dictum that his films are not roundtable debates, discusses *Bad Guy* with critic Volker Hummer*, let me clear up that "normal" entails no value judgement. I simply mean that it is the norm ruling this particular world.

Kim has told us repeatedly that to him making films is an attempt at understanding life. Again, "life" here is not a grand word. Understanding life is the *raison d'être* of philosophy, and he has also made it clear that he does not intend to become a philosopher. Then we had

---

* http://archive.sensesofcinema.com/contents/01/19/ kim_ki-duk.html, last visited January 2009.

better think in terms of individual life and its enigmas. The phrase *"They live asking the same questions I am asking"* marks a difference between the undifferentiated "they" and this director. "They" tend to be paralyzed in thought, or try to provide answers through art and science, while Kim transforms his questions into films. Probably he comes up with an answer after the process of writing, shooting, and editing is over. Still, it is his personal answer, and he does not share it with the spectator, who is free to reach his own conclusions or to remain in ignorance.

Bad Guy is a stark story about a thug who makes a living by pimping women and who has no moral restraints whatsoever. In psychoanalytical terms, one could say his superego is in abeyance. In ordinary language, the superego could be loosely equated to the notion of "conscience," the little internal voice that reminds us of the barriers separating right and wrong. Hang-gi (the thug) grabs what catches his fancy, and in the film the object of his desire is not a "what" but a "she," an educated girl who knows nothing of the marginal world. The extraordinary thing is that, rather than treasuring his object for his own pleasure, he pimps her out, and finds his solace watching her through a grimy windowpane. Let us not go any further. If this has aroused your interest, please watch the movie.

Anyway, in his interview with Hummer, Kim makes the questions that triggered this film explicit. Why, if we are all born equal, society divides us into classes that are not able to interact? Is there a chance of changing this?

He also adds one more element to his theory of language by explaining violence as a manner of language that surfaces in the face of impotence or after having been unable to prevent verbal and/or physical abuse. It would seem that someone who has been "betrayed" through language—who has been lied to, for example—gives it up as a useless, contemptible tool and begins to express his feelings through blunt, forceful action.

As in all of Kim's films, the aesthetic treatment blends with the baseline story. Exception made of certain scenes, and always for a reason, darkness or semi-darkness predominates. There are startling games of reflection in glass, mirrors, or surfaces that serve as such. Paintings by Schiele (d. 1918) crudely fix the images of the drab brothel life. The film gives no respite.

The spectator may or may not ask himself the same questions that haunted the director. I would venture to say that in a non-Asian environment and, again, with exceptions, for Asia offers much diversity, the questions will be different. In the West, class mobility is no longer a matter of concern, and it is rare to find a class system so restrictive that it rather resembles Indian castes. What is definitely true is that those born below the poverty line seem condemned to a vicious circle that usually lands them in jail or in the morgue, for lack of access to the educational system heavily conditions any other upgrades in their future lives. But there is no doubt that questions will arise. Most importantly, the psyche of the characters and their interpersonal relations will set audiences thinking about whether they are watching a fantasy originated in the mind in one of the characters or a sick aspect of reality unfamiliar to them. Regardless of the nature of the questions, I gather that the director will be pleased by just knowing that he has given people a serious shake-up, and that they will have to try and reorganize a world that, by the end of the film, is standing upside down.

The Inside Story

In the *Special Features* section of the *3-Iron* (2004) DVD released by Sonny Pictures Classic, Kim Ki Duk speaks about the making of this particular film, though one might well apply his comments to his filmography in general.

Kim has a very pleasant, youthful voice and speaks with poise and confidence. He soliloquizes in Korean about various aspects of the "kitchen work" involved in production, and you are under the delusion that you "understand" directly from that faceless voice addressing you from the screen, when in fact, not knowing the language, you are reading subtitles.

From the very beginning, you experience a shock. In contexts other than this, Kim has laid emphasis on the idea of dreams, his own as a filmmaker and the frustrated ones of his characters. Now he is talking about money, and his approach to the subject is anything but romantic. This is in no way intended to be a derogatory remark. It just struck me as odd and admirable that somebody whose sensitivity turns even the crudest themes into works of art could be so cold-headed and practical.

As he shows parts of the movie, he explains that a low-budget film in Korea might cost between three and five million dollars, an unthinkable figure unless the film is backed by solid funding. In this particular case, a Japanese company provided half the money, and the actors and crew, director included, agreed not to collect a fee for their work, establish a cooperative, and cross their fingers hoping that the film would do well enough to distribute the earnings among the partners.

Kim candidly says that he does not cast well-known actors into his films both because they are not agreeable to this kind of deal and because they are not happy to appear in films that are poorly distributed in Korea. Believe it or not, his films have a faithful yet small following in the country, whereas they are big blockbusters in Europe and the United States. This is partly in keeping with his answer to my question about his choice of actors:

> *I don't think there are actors just right for my films. Whoever understands my scenario and timing is possible to cast. It's more important to me to show my films as if in documentary rather than with famous actors who may be able to do well in the box-office. Before considering actors, I always focus on my screen play/scenario. If a director is a painter, scenario is a brush and actors are like tubes of colors. It doesn't mean that the painter's role is bigger than tubes of colors.*

Timing is essential to the budget. Kim shoots his films in record time, between eleven and fourteen days. He points out that *Spring, Summer, Autumn, Winter . . . and Spring* took longer: twenty days. Taking such care about how the money available is spent, Kim is extraordinarily resourceful. He does not do reshoots, and if some minor detail goes wrong in the first shoot, he makes a small change in the next scene so that nobody will notice and it will fit naturally into the storyline. Besides, unlike most directors, who shoot scenes taking place in the same location all at once, regardless of where they come in the script, Kim shoots sequentially, developing the plot from beginning to end. Thus he may have to return to one location on several occasions. In *3-Iron* he used his own motorbike, an impressive BMW, and even rode it himself in the takes where you can see what you think is the back of the male lead—who is in fact standing away from the eye of the camera.

Another funny trick that saved a lot of money in this film is the way in which he avoided renting a golf course. He tells that he used to practice hitting a golf ball by drilling a hole through it, pushing a long piece of string through the hole, and firmly securing the loose ends of the string in a knot around the bottom of a tree trunk. This is exactly what he makes his male lead do in the film. Kim plays "a little golf," emphatically denies that it is a bourgeois game, and finds it fascinating and frustrating at once. Since every time you are about to hit the ball you need to consider a new strategy, he says that you need to tackle each move with an empty mind, a disposition that resembles that of preparation for philosophical contemplation.

I found it intriguing that he prefers to work with photographers/cameramen with little experience. The explanation, though, was perfectly reasonable. A seasoned professional would probably try to impose his own angles and composition. Conversely, a less renowned photographer will take his cue from Kim so, in a way, the photography is his, vicariously. As for the editing, he thoroughly enjoys doing it himself.

That there are no special actors "just right for his films" is an understatement. He sometimes changes the script on the spur of the moment, just when they are about to shoot. Thus, the actors are bound to be pliable to forget the lines they have learned or the movements and body language they have rehearsed and adapt to the new idea without wasting time. The saying "time is money" and its strict application do not detract from the quality of these films.

The Reason for Existence

Of Kim Ki Duk's vast filmography (15 films in eleven years), two movies especially explore the whys and wherefores of human existence: *3-Iron* and *Spring, Summer, Autumn, Winter... and Spring*. Since we have gone over his work methodology by referring to the former, we may as well go into the story and the director's thoughts about it.

As happens with many writers, an insignificant personal experience triggers off Kim's imagination. When he developed *Bad Guy*, he had lived an unpleasant incident in the red-light district. In the case of *3-Iron*, on arriving home, he saw that someone had blocked the keyhole with a flyer. It occurred to him that this could be a clever ruse for a thief to spot whether the occupants were out of town. If the thief passed by the following day and the flyer had not been removed, he felt safe to break in.

However, the story in the film is very far removed from this initial thought. Keeping the flyer trick as a leitmotif for the first half or so of the film, Kim created a character that is true to life within the parameters of the film, but quite improbable in real life. (This is accounted for in a Groucho Review* to be cited later.)

A young college graduate plays this game, but he does not steal anything. He uses empty homes as a tempo-

---

* http://www.grouchoreviews.com/interviews/118, last visited January 2009.

rary abode, has a bath, takes his pick from well-stocked freezers or refrigerators, indulges in listening to what music is at hand, and occasionally sleeps over. In return for the hospitality unbeknownst to the owners/tenants, he fixes gadgets that are out of order. Once, he breaks into a house where an abused wife is nursing her grief, oblivious of doors, keyholes, and noises. Eventually she catches him out, and a strange atmosphere of relaxation and intimacy develops between them. The youngster leaves just as the husband is coming up the driveway. He suddenly has second thoughts about what may happen to the woman—after all, he has already seen the bruises on her face—and turns around his motorbike to confront the husband. From then on, the movie develops into an updated variety of magic realism, should such a thing exist.

In the interview mentioned above, Kim says, as usual, that this film poses some of the questions he keeps asking himself: what is life? Why are we in the world and what is the point of our being here? Yet more specifically, he narrows down the story to what he calls "an exercise in invisibility" and "the resolution of coexistence."*

The notion of "now you see me, now you don't" can be clearly inferred from the young man's presence in the empty houses. While it is true that he cannot be seen at the time when the occupants are away, they do not seem to realize that someone else has been tampering with their belongings, eating their food or, what is even

---

* Ibid.

more striking, that broken gadgets are now in perfect working order. Much, much later, along the lines of magic realism, these people claim to "feel" a presence that they cannot explain. The spectator is left to decide whether the youngster has returned a second time or whether his aura remained behind and is finally perceived by sensibilities that have perhaps been long numbed.

Moreover, there is no need to infer the "exercise in invisibility" from the scenes inside the prison. (Yes, the hero did spend some time in prison, as was to be expected.) He practices an illusion of invisibility in every possible way, failing and restarting until he finally succeeds in staying out of the line of vision. It is not surprising that the idea of perspective and of the 180 degrees that the human eye's range of vision can cover should occur to a painter. Well, a film director now, but once a painter, always a painter. The point of invisibility does not pose a problem with respect to others, but to ourselves. I do not know whether this question also haunts Kim. The reflected images that appear also in this film might suggest that the question works both ways. We cannot really see ourselves, and the mirror or makeshift mirror returns an inverted image, an inverted "self."

The issue of coexistence is a harder nut to crack. In the interview, Kim first speaks of the youngster and the husband as real people, and says that the open ending gives them the possibility of finding some manner of coexistence. But then he proposes that

each other is a figment of each other's imagination
and fantasy [. . .] To the husband, both of them
could actually be figments of his imagination—his
fantasy. *

Seen thus, the spectator is called upon to make a decision about what he/she is watching. Films move on
fleetingly, and there is no time to focus on the action
and ponder the metaphysical nuances that the story may
or may not convey. Perhaps you need to revisit the film
in your mind, and then you come to a different conclusion. If the two male characters are parts of a whole, if
one is the other's fantasy, or an ideal/coveted/feared
aspect of the same subject, coexistence is mandatory.
Conscious or unconscious refusal to coexist with his
other selves would plunge the character headlong into
schizophrenia.

At the end of the interview, to define the tension
between opposites in his movies, Kim says something
that linguistics posited many years ago in the area of
semantics, among others. Great minds do think alike,
only Kim, because of the ". . . always a painter," exempli-
fies his stance through colors.

This is sort of a kind of philosophy of mine, but
it's this idea that the colors of black and white are
actually the same color. You can only explain black

---

* Ibid.

*by pointing to what's white. You can only explain
white by pointing to what's black.*

Spring, Summer, Autumn, Winter ... and Spring is
the other film that Kim mentioned in relation to the
mysteries of human existence. Many critics call this film
a "Buddhist fable." The reason why the word "fable" is
used to describe it escapes me, for even though it makes
a cautionary point about the ages of man, the speaking
animals that characterize the genre are nowhere to be
found. It is true that the monk uses animals as living
teaching resources in an effort to give his ward an object lesson that will drive wisdom into his senses more
forcefully and lastingly than words. Still, if I were given
the chance to choose a descriptive phrase, I would rather
call it an "allegory." This film, neatly divided into the
seasons chosen for the title, tells the story of childhood,
adolescence, youth, maturity, and old age mingled with
the affects (both positive and negative) that accompany
each stage of development. Moral issues are presented
in oppositive pairs: joy and sorrow, guilt and atonement,
spiritual blindness and awareness, and death and rebirth.
Perhaps I should make it clear that my choice of the
adjective "oppositive" rather than "opposite" is due to
the fact that the constituents of the pairs do not actually
stand in opposition to each other, but rather indicate a
position in a relative continuum. As a matter of fact, at
least in some versions of Buddhism, each constituent is
the necessary consequence of the previous state. Besides,
this view is in agreement with Kim's idea of explaining

white by contrast to black; in other words, it would be impossible to make a distinction between the elements of the pairs if one went missing.

The apparent story tells of an orphaned child raised by a monk in a wild, secluded area surrounded by water (which must be understood as a metaphor too, as water is a source of life and/or death in all myths and religions) and accessed by two huge doors with scary allegoric figures painted on them. Hard as the monk tries to discipline the boy and make him abide by at least five of the many Buddhist principles, from the very start he is not persuaded that his disciple will have the strength to renounce the world.

The teachings of the Buddha that Kim (born a Catholic) seems to have slipped into the movie are the following:

Life as we know it ultimately is or leads to suffering in one way or another.

Suffering is caused by craving or attachment to worldly pleasures of all kinds.

This is often expressed as a deluded clinging to a certain sense of existence, to selfhood, or to the things of people that we consider the cause of happiness or unhappiness.

Suffering ends when craving ends as one is freed from desire.

This is achieved by eliminating all delusion, thus reaching a liberated state of enlightenment.

Reaching this liberated state is achieved by following the path laid out by the Buddha.

The statue of the Buddha presides over the plain temple with its small adjoining rooms where master and disciple live, and prayers and libations are regularly offered to the statue. In time, when it looks as if the boy has been drained of the natural passion for inquiry and discovery that characterizes a healthy childhood, desire, craving, and suffering arrive in the disguise of a young girl who suffers from a strange ailment of the soul and is left with the monk in the hope that he will cure her.

I cannot guess what would cross the mind of an Asian audience when the pale, skinny, fainting girl makes her appearance. But I do remember that where I saw this film, a Municipal Cultural Center located at Buenos Aires University, the people in the room burst out laughing. I think we could read each other's thoughts. No one believed for a moment that she suffered from an ailment of the soul. Quite the contrary, we were convinced that she pined for very physical reasons; that she was nostalgic about something she had not yet experienced. Be it as it may, the girl gets cured after losing her virginity to the young man, leaves, he follows her into the evil city, and you can imagine the rest from the oppositive pairs discussed above. A better alternative is to see the movie, for the beauty of its scenery and the changing seasons are truly unmatched.

The monk's attitude is rather confusing. He must know what is going on between the two young people, and it should be his moral duty to stop it. On the other hand, perhaps he too thought that the only effective cure lay in what the Buenos Aires audience anticipated, and thus let Nature follow its course against the Buddha's best advice. Without taking positive action, the monk utters a hair-raising prophecy: "Lust awakens the desire to possess which ends in the intent to murder."

Like Hitchcock, Kim seems to enjoy flaunting his presence in front of the cameras. In *3-Iron* he rode his motorbike. In *Spring, Summer . . .* he played the part of the monk in the *Winter* section of the film, allegedly because the actor who had been engaged for the job was unable to fulfill his commitment. (Another version has it that no actor was found to play the part.) I am told that he sang a little in another of his films and in the opening of a Czech film festival. He is, indeed, a man of many talents, and he garners international recognition for his originality, as we shall see when we list down the amazing number of nominations and awards that he earned.

The Pain of Reality

Having read something to the effect that Kim Ki Duk's latest movies are less focused on the raw aspects of life and that he has turned to depict such human traits as satisfy audiences' seeming need to find their "better selves" mirrored in films, I asked him whether this was true.

> *One may say that I have changed, but I am not so sure about that. I always keep in mind that I must not abandon my core belief depending on the opinion of the majority. It is said that my recent films are different from the earlier ones, but I think it is hidden. . . . If you look closer, these [recent] films are more cruel and sad, and I think that it is a way to reach self-realization beyond the sublime. Lately, I wonder if the reason movies' depiction of fantasy has deepened is because the pain of reality has gotten more severe. I remain unhappy . . . continue to be in the state of being more sad and lonely.*

I suspect that whoever wrote that Kim had mellowed his attitude did not see the films, and neither had I by the time I asked this question, the reason being that very few of his movies can be found in Argentina. In any case, that there has been a change is not "the opinion of the majority," though most probably the majority of the public would celebrate being spared the cruelty that confronts them from the screen.

The behavior of audiences offers an interesting, fertile field of analysis. When gross cruelty is portrayed in films, audiences tend to fill cinemas and enjoy severed limbs, hacked body parts bouncing around, fingernails being torn off with screwdrivers and the rest of the ghastly horrors that the geniuses of the genre so cleverly devise. This kind of cruelty does not bother audiences because they know too well that it belongs in a Disney world, "a Barnum and Bailey world, just as phony as it could be." They feel so detached from what they are watching and so sure that they would be incapable of torturing/murdering anybody so heinously in real life that they show a high threshold of tolerance to the images on the screen.

On the other hand, everyday forms of brutality such as battering and rape and subtle yet heart-rending forms of psychological cruelty remarkably lower the threshold of tolerance. Even if these audiences do not practice any form of cruelty—an arguable matter, but beyond the scope of these lines—they know, deep down in their hearts, that they could, given a slight change of circumstances, become victims, victimizers, or both. The not necessarily conscious fear of what the self can be prompted to do and/or to endure induces a feeling of utter rejection of forms of cruelty closer to reality.

Because I do not think comparisons would be fair here, I will refrain from expounding on the theories and works authored by Alfred Jarry*, Antonin Artaud†, and Fernando Arrabal‡. When Kim says "*I must not abandon my core belief*," he is reminding us of the existential and metaphysical questions that he cannot put out of his mind, and of the fact that this is why he makes movies. It could be said that he challenges audiences to follow his quest, even though he must be well aware that, generally speaking, movie audiences go to the cinema to have a good time and forget about their troubles, so they are not thankful for leaving the cinema with a sore psyche and their brains turned upside down. Mass audiences love being spoon-fed, while Kim is determined not to relent in his struggle to encourage some ulterior thinking.

We would have to discuss the films prior to deciding on their being "more cruel and more sad." Perhaps what he calls "hidden" is that there is less physical violence and a lot more psychical torture and self-inflicted torture. One thing that confirms the sadness in these films is that some of the earlier ones ended on a note of hope after the characters had been through purgatory or hell. In the most recent films, it looks as if psychic wounds have

---

* French writer and playwright, 1873–1907. Best known for his delusional theory of pataphysics, his plays illustrating his ideas are considered surrealistic to the point of cruelty.

† French playwright, actor, poet, and theater director, 1896–1948. Creator of "The theater of cruelty." In his theory, "cruelty" does not always mean what we usually understand by it. Nonetheless, his ideas to subject audiences to certain experiences still prove quite disturbing.

‡ Spanish poet, screenwriter, playwright, novelist, and film director, 1932–. A follower of Jarry and Artaud.

no chance of healing, and what is broken will remain broken forever.

One example of this is *Time* (2006), a very complex movie about a love relationship that could stand for all love relationships involving people between their late twenties and early thirties. In the case of *Time*, the spectator is also given the choice of accepting that all that he sees is actually happening or else take it as a metaphor of encounter and disenchantment.

In this film, the female lead becomes insanely jealous of a woman with whom her boyfriend exchanges cards for the insurance company after a fender-bender in the busy city traffic. She persecutes him verbally in every possible way, to the extent of asking him to think of the stranger while making love to her. Of course, as should be expected from every genuine hysteric, when he admits that he has taken her clue just to please her, she flies into a rage, and leaves his apartment when he finally drops off to sleep. While they were still arguing in bed, she ranted about his being bored with her body, particularly her face. The boyfriend feels terribly confused: he has not really taken notice of the other girl's face, but such insistance on his girl-friend's part ends up by making him wonder whether he has or he has not.

On waking up the following morning, Jiwoo (the boyfriend), thinking that this a lovers' tiff like others they may have had in their long relationship, tries to have it out with Sehie (the girl-friend) at her workplace and her apartment. He is deeply astonished to find that Sehie has disappeared from her usual whereabouts without leaving any traces.

Jiwoo goes through disbelief, frustration, feelings of having been betrayed in his love, melancholy, anger . . . the list is long. He keeps chasing her shadow in a café, half hoping that, if she ever returns, she will make her comeback there. Some recurrent comic incidents along the lines of slapstick comedy in the café relieve the tension of a wait that seems pointless.

In a parallel time, Sehie cuts pieces of different faces out of magazines and makes an appointment with a plastic surgeon. The surgeon does his best to discourage her from having an operation, and warns her that she will not recover before six months, but she will not budge: she wants a completely different face.

She spends the following six months spying on Jiwoo, and as soon as her face has healed goes after him. They engage in a relationship in which Jiwoo is clearly at a disadvantage, although they share magic moments of happiness and companionship. Saehie (the name Sehie adopted along with her new persona) taunts him by asking him what he will do if his old lover returns. "She will not," replies Jiwoo. "But what if she does?" retorts Saehie. And that same morning she leaves a note signed "Sehie" on the windshield of Jiwoo's car. From there on, there evolves a sick game of masks, deceit, mental torture, and immense suffering.

Critic Darcy Paquet* says that the "characters' actions

---

* http://www.koreanfilm.org/kfilm06.html#time, last visited January 2009.

violate psychological norms." To begin with, there is no such thing as "psychological norms." There are psychiatric descriptors in the DSM IV, listing and labeling 297 disorders. However, the psyche does not follow norms; if it did, it would be child's play to "fix" it.

If you choose to view the film as a metaphor on the impossibility of encounter, you will be startled to find that if love depends on visual recognition of physical features, love itself is a mystification. Sehie bought herself a new face, but not a new voice, a new body, or a new skin. What happened to Jiwoo's tactile and auditory memory of a woman to whom he had talked and made love for so long? In their determination to take the story to the letter, will sticklers for "psychological norms" argue that he suffers from prefrontal cortex and auditory apparatus impairment?

Yes, the cruelty and the sadness are less obvious than in the "thugs" films. But they are there all right, together with a challenge to those who are comfortably installed in the belief that true love, once found, may be taken for granted. What is "true love," anyway? Each individual loves in a different way, and conflict and suffering arise when we want to be loved exactly as we love. So perhaps it would be wiser to let sleeping dogs lie? This is not Kim's way. His questions awake the dormant dogs in us, and I guess this is one of the reasons why his films are so strongly resisted by some audiences and critics.

"*The pain of reality has gotten more severe.*" The word "reality" points to too many doors. On the one hand, we live in the bubble of our personal reality, where the temperature keeps changing all the time, all the more so if we are very sensitive. On the other hand, the bubble is transparent, so we cannot help seeing the deterioration of the world outside, and our suffering increases accordingly. Excruciating pain occurs when external reality pierces the bubble's walls, preventing us from differentiating between the outside and the inside. When this happens, we are invaded by universal suffering, and find ourselves unable to fight such a powerful army of horrors. We no longer distinguish the boundaries between the self and the external world. We starve with the underfed, die with the casualties of wars we cannot even begin to understand, weep with the widows, the orphans, the maimed, and the homeless. Depending on our psychopathological structure, we sink into impotence, rage, depression or a combination of the three in which each of these affects takes turns at becoming dominant, with nefarious consequences to our lives.

Kim says that he probably takes refuge in fantasy because of the severity of the pain. Yet there is nothing "fantastic"—in the sense of "imaginary"—in these recent movies. Reality has been aesthetically transformed into an object of art, but Kim's films do not go beyond magic realism, as I have remarked earlier on. There is a clue that suggests this in *Time*, in a scene at a bar where Jiwoo and his friends are discussing what books they read. Someone mentions García Márquez's *One Hundred Years of Solitude**. I do not think this is a random choice.

---

* García Márquez, Gabriel. *Cien años de soledad*; Editorial Sudamericana, Buenos Aires, 1968.

An anonymous Italian physician told me a few days ago that people do not seem to realize that this book is about one man's mind, or psyche, if you will. It is not usually seen in that light. Most ordinary readers take it as a divertimento, something that not even Kim's worst detractors would venture to call his films.

Sad Dream, released in 2008, seems to be the most daring of Kim's insights into the connection between reality and fantasy. It points to the irrationality of the rational, with a single identity split between two bodies, one of them acting out what the other dreams in his sleep. Laden with universal symbols, this movie will undoubtedly provide food for thought to all kinds of audiences. It definitely gives a startling twist to the equation posed in many of his previous works.

A working biography is not supposed to include any information irrelevant to the subject's career. The trouble is that Kim's career is not about technical decisions. Lenses, cameras, and technology are the tools of his trade, but they would be completely useless if there were not a non-material core: his feelings. Hence it would be an error to overlook the last sentence in his answer.

"I remain unhappy . . . continue to be in the state of being more sad and lonely." A few years ago I engaged in an acrimonious argument with a would-be adolescent musician who flew into a tantrum at my saying that great works of art resulted from their creators' irreparable sadness and loneliness. In his *Ethics*, Aristotle states that the pursuit of happiness takes a lifetime. Moreover, he does

not assure that happiness will be achieved in the end. So we are left with the unsavory conclusion that happiness is not a state, but a pursuit, not because Aristotle said so, but because our daily life confirms it. We enjoy brief spells of happiness, and when they are over—too quickly, alas—we return to the pursuit which, in artists, is the stuff of their works.

Consciousness of loneliness is the privilege and the curse of the sensitive. All human beings are intrinsically lonely, although few are aware of it. And of those who are, particularly if their name often makes the headlines, few if any will drop the mask of happiness and bliss that the public mistakes for their real faces. It takes great courage and honesty to admit that you are sad and lonely despite the enormous success you have earned worldwide. Kim is one of those rare "winners" whose truthfulness in creation is consistent with his truthfulness in life.

The Bow (2005) is another of his recent films that belies the idea of a change of direction in his view of the world. Set within a confined environment with its particular rules like many of his other films, the movie tells the story of an elderly man who lives in a boat with a girl he has "adopted," planning to marry her when she is old enough. The bow can be used as a weapon or as a musical instrument, depending on how the string attached to it is handled. It is mostly used to keep at bay the young men who have designs upon the girl, but the elderly man's dreams of a perfect life with the girl become shattered as she grows into womanhood. The girl definitely does not relish the thought of spending the

rest of her days in the boat/prison with a father figure
turned husband/jailer.

*I don't think that it is desirable to receive many
questions about my movies. If it could just be
felt, understood, and shared, there is no need for
explanation.*

This quote appeared earlier in the text, but I feel it
necessary to revisit it in the context of *The Bow*. Some
critics, whose reviews can be accessed from Kim Ki
Duk's* website, did not ask questions, did not feel or
share, and understood accordingly.

We all have a right to our opinions. Still, if you are
familiar with an artist's work, it should strike you as
odd that he/she has suddenly fallen out of step with his
previous achievements. You must be missing something,
so you probably need to look again and try to find the
artist's soul beyond the seeming flatness of the story. In
the case of *The Bow,* issues such as a modernized version of the Pygmalion myth are staring you in the face.
It does not matter whether or not Kim was familiar with
the myth. (Let us remember that he said he was not
interested in learning much about European/American
languages and culture.) Mythemes are universal, as
is the collective unconscious. Seen thus, perhaps *The
Bow* takes on new meanings that will pass unnoticed if,
following Kim's technique of the confined environment,

---

* http://koreanfilm.org/kimkiduk.html, last visited January 2009.

you encage your analysis into the Korean culture with Buddhist or pseudo-Buddhist legends.

This leads to a question about the need to "analyze" a work of art. According to Kim, the answer is a categorical "no!" My personal feeling is that these analyses tend to dissect the work into neatly labeled fragments until you are left with a handful of boxes from which the original art has fled. However, this is how critics and reviewers earn their living, and their practice is undeniably legitimate. But if the phrase "appreciation of art," coined long ago in British universities, replaced the coldness of the "analysis" with its laboratory connotations, perhaps it would be easier to retain the art.

Relationships and Individuals

When I asked Kim what he would like to convey as an artist, free association streamed in a most rewarding manner:

> *The world that we live in is already based on an accomplice relationship. Often we divide people into the good and the bad, but I don't believe in such a thing. We [are destined to] live mirror-like life existences. In the history of humankind, many things about life we want to correct and right, but still we continue to fight over petty little things.*
>
> *Now I want to talk about an individual happiness and freedom above happiness for the majority or a country. That happiness is not just material happiness, but happiness repeated (and sustained) by (true) wisdom and awareness. Every day, through awakening through new knowledge and awareness one reaches a state [beyond the world we live in].*

This answer sounds like a movie in its own right, because of the disquieting thoughts it triggers. What are we accomplices to? Is Kim pointing to social injustice, to a state of things in which a relatively small number of well-fed people turn their backs on the needy? To the blindness evidenced by our overexploitation of natural resources while the self-appointed organizations that claim to protect the environment join in its systematic depletion? To the pointless wars staged by greedy politicians in connivance with arms manufacturers and based on blatant lies that none of us bothers to challenge? To the breach of human rights in the name of democracy, a fallacy that the majority condones for the sake of "personal safety"? To the schemes that bar the kind of education that will help our children make useful contributions to fast-moving developments in all fields, with older generations staunchly advocating the "good old ways"? To all of the above?

Kim does not talk about politics. However, man is a political animal (Aristotle again, *Politics*). Without going into the complicated developments that justify this statement, we can resort to one quote that may suit our purpose. "A constitution is just when it benefits everyone in the city and unjust when it benefits only those in power." Replacing the notion of "constitution" for that of "government/administration/society," and bearing in mind that, whatever the form of government, its active supporters will live more comfortably than the rest of the population, perhaps the kind of relation Kim is thinking of will become clearer.

"Accomplice" is a hard word thrust down our throats. It makes us partners in crime, the sort of crime that is not contemplated in any legal system, since the systems themselves are, in this sense, accomplices of the evils of this world. In other words, politics is failing badly.

Kim's disbelief in the division of people between

"good" and "bad" brings to light a simplification that has eased man's conscience for ages. In our global civilization, the "good" follow into the footsteps of opinion leaders and politically correct chieftains, pay their taxes, stick to the positions assigned to them in the assembly line of mass consumption and mass culture. The "bad," on the other hand, do not abide by the law, a fact that turns them into undesirables, outcasts, or criminals, as the case may be. Still, the "bad" have codes, and there is method to their marginality. The "good" do not understand either the codes or the method, and would feel relieved if the "bad" were sealed into a sack and thrown into the high seas. For lack of that option, they content themselves with a severe prison system. What Kim has been trying to show, with varying degrees of success (not because of his devices, but because of the difficulty in changing deeply rooted beliefs), is that bad and good coexist in one and the same person. This is not great news: all religions talk about these two forces struggling in and for the soul. The most successful ones, like the Christian varieties, endeavor to persuade men that the choice is theirs, forewarning them that it is not a one-time choice, but that they will have to lean to one side or the other before every decision in their lives, no matter how small. When Kim presents his "bad" characters, like Crocodile and the ruthless pimp in *Bad Guy*, he endows them with tiny traces of a rough sort of kindness or, in the latter case, with whatever positive evolution is possible given the chasms that vomited them and let them loose into the realm of the "good." Definitely, "bad" and "evil" do not mean the same, and his characters may be rogues, wrongdoers, criminals, amoral, but not truly evil, for the simple reason that evilness requires consciousness of the difference with good. These characters do not know what good is, so they would not define themselves as evil, and who are we to judge? Furthermore, "good" and "bad," like the rest of our description of man and the world, are related to a convention agreed upon by the majority. As far back as 1726, Jonathan Swift, Doctor of Divinity, published *Gulliver's Travels*. General consensus has it that Swift intended the book to reflect a political satire or parody of recent and current political and social issues in England, but what stands out is in fact that different societies uphold different conventions, so what is "good" in some will be "bad" in others. In a way, the existence of contrastive behaviors is a repetition of Kim's definition of color: "[. . .] You can only explain black by pointing to what's white. You can only explain white by pointing to what's black."

His other concern in this respect is that we tend to judge from appearances. The "good" will not look beyond a man's shabby clothes, disheveled hair, and stubbly chin to find a fellow being that deserves respect as such. Kim demands respect for the human condition, a stand that few seem ready to embrace.

The mirror-like existences which, in his opinion, we are destined to live suggest several lines of thought. One is that the people at the bottom of the social ladder (the "bad") mirror the ways of those at the top, but as they come from different places and have not been

blessed with the same opportunities, the image becomes distorted and grotesque, as in funfair mirrors.
Another is that we strive hard to reach uniformity so
that we all look a reflection of our neighbor. Through
lack of an "original," of "the real thing," infinite mirrors
placed across from each other repeat the same image.
This second notion would free us from responsibility,
since we would then be mere "copies" of other copies. I
think this is in keeping with Kim's belief that mankind
has failed to right its wrongs. There have been great
men and women, but not societies composed in their
entirety by great individuals. One swallow does not
make a summer, and man's nature is, unfortunately,
petty and self-centered. What are the "little things" we
fight for? Power, money, fame, and success. In the plan
of the universe—supposing there is one—these are
indeed little things. However, I love the Amazon.com
advertising of David Grinspoon's *Lonely Planet: The
Natural Philosophy of Alien Life**: are we part of the plan
of the universe or some freak of circumstance? If, to our
disappointment, we were to find the second alternative
to be true, the little things we fight for would take on a
different dimension. "Every man for himself," which is
what has been happening ever since the earliest times,
would make perfect sense.

Kim claims that he is no philosopher, but his remarks
on happiness, wisdom, and awareness belie him. It is
precisely the philosopher who wants to talk/write about

---

* No publisher or date of publication provided.

"happiness repeated (and sustained) by (true) wisdom and awareness," and it is interesting to remember that in Buddhism, freedom does not refer to "freedom of rights" but to freedom of desire. Material happiness achieved through access to all the comforts that make our lives easier and more pleasurable are difficult to forego inside a consumer society. The malady of status seeking seems to have infected all social layers, to the extent that those whose meager economic resources prevent them for purchasing "the real thing" (a Rolex watch, for example) will settle for a cheap replica. Sociologists account for this phenomenon by saying that ostentation of fake valuable objects compensates for both material and spiritual lacks. At the other end of the spectrum, incredibly rich people do not hesitate to buy valuables such as priceless paintings stolen from museums and enjoy them in secrecy and solitude. Donald Duck's Uncle Scrooge lives in the real world.

That *"through awakening through new knowledge and awareness one reaches a state [beyond the world we live in]"* entails a step into spirituality that honors Kim's positive view of mankind. Although he makes it clear that these ideas apply to the individual and not to the majority, finally a summation of individuals will yield a majority, a society, or a country.

It is not at all easy to awaken to new knowledge and awareness. You need an inclination to grasp what the world has to offer, look inside you and outside at the same time, find the internal cause, and experience the joy of humble tasks.

In the last few years, some nine-day wonder charlatans appropriated the concept of the internal cause and integrated it into their "miraculous" recipes for instant happiness. I was delighted to find that the internal cause and its simultaneous internal effect lie at the heart of Buddhism. Very briefly put, with my apologies, because I am not an expert in Buddhism, it is said that we make causes* in everything we do, say, and think. Every cause we make anticipates its effect in our future lives, although we know nothing of it until the time comes for the effect to emerge. This means that we often mistake the cause for the effect. For example, if our spouse runs off with another man/woman, we tend to believe that their relationship is the cause and our spouse leaving us is the effect. But we have probably had profound disagreements before the third party appeared, in which case the disagreements are the cause, and our spouse getting involved with someone else is the effect. If we carefully explore our feelings, actions, and utterances, we can change the deeply hidden cause and prevent its future negative effect. Although Kim, as I have said before, is not a Buddhist, I believe that the state he speaks of, rising above the world we live in, is very much connected to the above concept, and that a closer look at some of his films reveals this principle at work.

---

* http://www.sgi-uk.org/index.php/buddhism/9thconsciousness, last visited January 2009.

Self Containment

Comfortably settled into the present, Kim is not interested in revisiting the past. When asked whether he thought it would have been easier for him to make headway in his career had he undergone formal training, he replied,

I cannot return now to that thought [of pondering whether more training would've made my journey as a director easier]. And I am satisfied with my expressions now.

I didn't learn systematically the filmmaking process, but within time, I learned about humans and their lives as well as various mechanical techniques. I believe that within a mechanical principle there lies a human principle and that within the nature's mystery, there lies human sensibility. My most important and fundamental teacher is nature.

If I had to study and memorize boring European cinematic history, either I might have ended up being like other directors or not become a director at all. I want to simply express freely within the limits of my own knowledge and experience.

I am truly happy for the fact that I do not know about a lot of things.

In a joke that combines psychoanalysis and grammar, language teachers have nicknamed the Type III Conditional "the neurotic tense." Indeed, such contrary to fact utterances as "If I had done/not done [something], I would/could/might/should have done [something better] [replace 'done' with whichever past participle you like]" is a neurotic trap that few of us manage to avoid. We tend to assess our successes and failures by looking back into past events along the road we walked that led us to where we are now. Kim definitely has escaped the trap, and lives the present to the full, with an eye in the future, as we have seen from what he wants to convey in his future works.

That he is *"satisfied with my* [his] *expressions now"* fills us with the hope that some day we will be able to say the same. It is well known that most creators declare to the media that their best work is the one to come, and that when they admit to being satisfied with a finished work, self-content reaches them *post factum.*

I imagine that learning about humans and their lives must have been preceded by or coexisted with a process of self-exploration and emotional growth and development. The wise inscription "Know thyself" on the front of Apollo's temple in Delphi enveloped a multiplicity of meanings by way of warning to those who came to the oracle in search of answers. No doubt Kim's alertness to his surroundings, combined with his acute power of observation, enabled him to learn more about humans than other less sensitive, more intellectual people would have picked up from books. Still, the "white–black" contrast applies, for you need internal parameters to contrast with what you see and sense behind the disguises people adopt in their public and private lives.

In this text, we have often spoken about masks: the ones used in many of the films as props standing for metaphors, and the ones cast off by the characters in an attempt to change their lives. T.S. Eliot's lines "To prepare a face to meet the faces that you meet"* points exactly to that, to the insincerity of relationships and to the masks suitable for concealing the real faces behind them. That Kim succeeded in learning about humans without being misled by the masks tells us of systematic work performed on himself as well as on his fellow-beings, and suggests that in this point, like in so many others, we can trust his judgement.

Kim professes to like *"analog story telling but, at times, when [digital] graphics are needed,"* he does not hold any biases against using them: *"My recent films have been utilizing some of those techniques."* Of course, analog technologies are far cheaper, but they also carry only so much information.

His view of mechanical principles sounds rather intriguing to the Occidental mind. (And perhaps to the Oriental mind as well, for Kim is every inch an independent thinker.) We tend to believe that mechanical principles underlie the functions of mechanical tools. While it is true that every tool has been devised by a human being, we do not think that the principle on

---

* T.S. Eliot, *The Love Song of J. Alfred Prufrock*, 1917.

which it works has been contrived by humans, but rather discovered by them. Embedded in Physics, mechanical principles came to light thanks to the observation and experiments carried out by outstanding scientists, such as Galileo, Newton, and Einstein, to mention just a few classical names, and were later expanded into quantum mechanics for processes at molecular and (sub)atomic levels. Incidentally, Galileo and Newton did not call themselves "scientists," for the word was coined in 1833. They were well trained in the basic disciplines of the times (Philosophy, Mathematics, Physics) and put them to good use in an effort to understand the laws of the universe. Man's thirst for knowledge and passion to dominate forces whose effects could be perceived but not explained may account for the human principle (curiosity and the will to prevail) that Kim refers to.

As for human sensibility lying within the mystery or mysteries of Nature, the Occidental mind would feel equally puzzled. We do not tend to establish a link between sensibility and Nature, although we certainly are sensitive to the manifestations of Nature, sometimes in wonder and others in awe. Rather, man has become intrinsically dissociated from Nature, and what used to be considered mysterious is now a matter of study for scientists. They tell us that just as the old mysteries involving the movements of the planets, the tides, vegetation, the countless forms of life, and so many others have been explained through the physical, chemical, and biological laws that rule Nature, so the time will come when mysteries yet unsolved will be cracked.

I agree that this approach sounds cold and matter-of-fact. Kim's belief is much more romantic and appealing. Moreover, in a world that has persuaded itself of its mastery and rights over nature, it is comforting to hear someone upholding a radically different view.

Perhaps Kim is expressing, with the economy of language that characterizes him, something similar to what Tagore wrote in his typical florid style:

> Must the sword rule for ever and not the sceptre? We feel the withering fierceness of the spirit of modern civilization, because it beats directly against our human sensibility; and it is we of the Eastern hemisphere who have the right to say that those who represent this great age of opportunities are furiously building their doom by their renouncement of the divine ideal of personality, for the ultimate in man is not in his intellect or material wealth: it is in his imagination of sympathy, in his illumination of heart, in his activities of self-sacrifice, in his capacity for extending love far and wide across all barriers of caste and colour, in his realizing this world not as a storehouse of mechanical power, but a habitation of man's soul with its eternal music of beauty and its inner light of a divine presence.*

---

* Rabindranath Tagore, *Construction versus Creation*, lecture published in Vol. VI of *The English Writings of Rabindranath Tagore*, New Delhi, Atlantic, 2007.

How did Kim, a city dweller, a man whose art leads to a final product that cannot do without technology, learn so much from Nature? We need to look at his choice of settings and locations in films such as *Spring, Summer, Autumn, Winter . . . and Spring* (there are others) to accept that while the learning process has not been revealed to us, it proved a complete success. In these movies, Nature and man play complementary roles, and we would not conceive of one without the other.

Self-made Kim Ki Duk, an admirer of some European films, as evidenced by the three movies that dramatically changed the course of his life, expresses his opinion about the history of European cinema in plain English. I would venture to say that what put him off was the studying and memorizing, for he is a doer, a creator, and a thinker, but did not feel cut out for going through the mill of academic life. He seems to suggest that other directors bear the mark of their alma mater; that all who have trained at film schools work in the same way and are barely distinguishable from one another. That he might not have become a director at all if he had followed the "disciplined" path speaks of a free spirit that refuses to be reined in by curricular agendas not his own.

We have seen that he paid dearly for his independent will (the films that he had to throw away). Still, far from feeling discouraged, he never sheepishly joined what he viewed as the beaten track, and it is patent that public recognition and international awards have proved him right. He is perfectly content *"within the limits of my* [his] *own knowledge and experience,"* only there is a catch

in this phrase. Kim continues to expand his limits, and there is even rumor that he may soon be invited to shoot in Hollywood. He does not seem reluctant at the idea, which arouses great expectancy in the cinematic milieu. Everybody wonders about the compatibility between a maverick filmmaker and the studio executives, who will surely strive hard to have their say on Kim's decisions.

I suspect that the last part of the answer—*"I am truly happy for the fact that I do not know about a lot of things"*—is far from naive. At the very least, it implies that we will understand that the lot of things he is happy not to know about are what he considers useless, trifling items of information that would take up storage space in his memory when he can put this space to better use. On the other hand, "knowing little" ensures that no unconsciously absorbed ideas will worm their way into Kim's legitimately original productions.

Although Kim shoots only his own screenplays, he appreciates and enjoys the diversity of movies made around the world.

To me, there are lots of diverse and cool films in the world (including independent films). Recently I watched via TV "Tuya's Marriage" by Wang Quan-An, and it was really remarkable. Through films like this, I am studying another [facade] of truth.

A film that Kim calls remarkable and educational for his purpose of exploring other aspects of truth must indeed be something to pay attention to. I surfed the web to find out about Mr. Wang and this particular movie, and found, to my surprise, that he is a very young sixth-generation Chinese film director born in 1965, and that *Tuya's Marriage* won the Golden Bear at the 2007 Berlin Film Festival.

Interestingly enough, this film centers around a woman who is surrounded by well-meaning yet incompetent men. Set in the Mongolian countryside as homage to Wang's Mongolian ancestors, the film lays emphasis on Tuya's full commitment to her family, composed of a disabled husband and two children. The seeming message of the film seems to be that it takes two—a husband and a wife—to run a home and do the rural work on which they live. Tuya is a resourceful, determined woman who tries to get help from a number of "suitors" swarming around her, but much as they love her, they prove as useless as her husband after the accident that deprived him of the use of his legs.

The next thing I wondered was what other aspects of truth this kind of film could reveal to Kim. The answer appears rather obvious, as none of his movies deals with housewives struggling to keep their family together. Also, on the rare occasions when Kim brushes on it, the institution of marriage is not shown as a desirable goal, but rather as a burden. If Kim is discovering/acknowledging the importance of women as pillars of the family and hints at their nurturing role in society in future films, the numbers of his female admirers will grow exponentially. It would be a great opportunity for those who dub him an anti-feminist to review his past works and accept that he is not intent on demonizing women.

Anyway, Kim is not in the least concerned about what audiences of either sex may or may not think of his films so, unlike many other directors, he does not have a particular kind of audience in mind as he works. His efforts, he repeats once again, are focused on improving his own comprehension of the world through writing scenarios and making movies.

> *As I mentioned before, I want to make movies about ironies of life I feel as I live.*
>
> *Audience is all an illusion. I think there is no substance. We are dragged on by the majority [opinions], which create another majority of sort, and then become slaves to that illusion. We shall not succumb to that illusion and true expressions persevere beyond that.*
>
> *I do not need slave audience that mob around like a school of fish. I want to communicate one-on-one through films.*
>
> *To me, it does not matter if that person [I want to communicate via film] is a Korean, an American, a European, an African, an Arab, or a South American—it does not matter.*

I read this statement as an artistic manifesto. The personal life stance in combination with a "we" poses a question that only Kim can answer. Is he mentally including other unnamed artists, or is it what we call "the Royal we"? In *Movements Made Manifest: The Prehistory of the Avant-Garde Manifesto**, Julian Hanna writes, "the manifesto has always [. . .] been about 'making enemies.' " Kim's disregard of audiences is consistent with his motives to make movies. Many great artists in the various fields of art have shown either indifference or antagonism—sometimes both—to actual and prospective audiences. Yet certain audiences, regardless of their likes or dislikes of an artist's works, contribute to the circulation of art. When an artist finds favor with these audiences, word of mouth will introduce his work into arts circuits, a fact that usually boosts financing of future productions. On the other hand, when audiences react negatively to the artist's work, extreme disapproval may also encourage the desire to see by themselves in certain individuals. This is what could give rise to the one-on-one communication that Kim aspires to, for there will always be individuals that stay out of the mainstream and appreciate what others are not ready to accept as art. In this sense, Kim stands as a one-man neo-avant-garde. But no matter what rights audiences think they have regarding the making or the crushing of an artist, they certainly resent being snubbed. I have already mentioned that there have been talks of Kim shooting a film in Hollywood. Should this happen, it would mean entering the film industry through the big door. However, the industry is about making money, not

---

* Julian Hanna, *The Prehistory of the Avant-Garde Manifesto*, http://www.arts.ed.ac.uk/europgstudies/rpropjects/avant-garde/ Edin%20abstract%2019.htm, last visited January 2009.

about promoting art, originality, or talent. These three factors tend to be regarded as extra bonuses. Money comes from movie theaters filled to capacity, and there seems to be a contradiction between Kim's admirably honest principles and the goals of the industry. It is not necessary to have a captive audience by catering to its dictates, but it may prove counterproductive to deny the substance of audiences. They are there all right, and once the work of art is released into the market, it is irretrievably lost to the artist; it does not belong to him anymore. It becomes immersed in the collective ownership of culture. From this point of view, it is true that the spectator's ethnic origin does not matter, but it is no less true that an American and an Arab, for example, do not share the same background either in terms of aesthetics or in their view of the world. Of course, there are exceptions. Still, there must surely be a way to reconcile Kim's universals with the standards of the different societies so that his movies may be a source of introspection to as many people as possible. They are too inspiring to remain confined to the small circuit of international festivals. It is both unfair and hard to believe that his films have garnered an impressive number of awards to end up as poor box-office prospects.

In this respect, it would seem as if Kim would rather break than bend. Speaking about the difficult relationship between him and audiences (including critics), he says,

Yes, there have been times I felt as my true quali-
ties [as a director] and meanings [of my films] were
not understood. But I realized quickly that such
things are unimportant. I cannot change who I am
because I am not recognized or appreciated [by
audience or critics]. More solidly, [it has made]
me insist upon my principles . . . making me more
stubborn. Hence, I think I am still able to make
films.

Movie making is one of the most costly en-
deavors. For 12 years I made 15 films, and not a
single film of mine has topped the box-office. But I
continue to make films and write screen plays. To
me, there is a world that exists just for my eyes to
see. I believe in it, and that path will lead me to
the path of overcoming it (obstacles) all.

This brings us back to the mainstream and the communication theory. Directors differ in style and origin,
and all of them have their strengths and their weak-
nesses. Kim's approach to filmmaking was commonly
found in the early days of the cinema, when there were
no instructors and no schools. In more recent times,
schools have proliferated everywhere, and non-ama-
teur directors either hold a degree or have worked long
years at photography or acting and closely watched the
ways of the directors under whom they worked, making
mental notes of the do's and don'ts. In any case, despite
their singularity, they could be classified into groups

according to a set of criteria: those who demand that
the script and their interpretation of it be followed to
the letter, those who encourage actors to improvise,
those who get involved in every aspect of the process,
and so forth. Each director makes his/her own choices,
and is generally (not always, mind) understood because
such choices are familiar to the mainstream audiences
and critics. Kim's choices need to be inferred from his
practice, and this is an effort that some people are not
willing to make while others simply lack the tools to
even start. Thus, perhaps more time will be required
for his qualities as a director to be properly understood.
Other innovators who refused to become part of the
herd underwent the same experience.

Regarding the meanings of his films, we are chal-
lenged by a language within a language. Kim's own
symbolic language, the product of his questions about
man and the world, is inserted into the language of
the cinema. Although movies shaped their distinct
language around the mid-twentieth century, it is still
hard for many people to grasp the "code." If they are
confronted with the additional difficulty of a "foreign"
language—foreign in the sense that the director avoids
conventional correspondence between the signifier and
the signified, encouraging audiences to metonymically
"slide" the signified—it is only natural that unexpected
meanings surface. Unexpected to Kim, that is. What he
meant to convey changed into something else as the
"sliding" took place.

It takes great fortitude to persist against all odds,

although it is not strictly true that Kim is "not recognized or appreciated." The impressive list of awards earned by some of his films shows that film festivals juries and audiences do recognize and appreciate his qualities. That none of his movies has topped the box-office is another cup of tea. Since he decided not to be a cog in the well-oiled machinery of the industry, his movies are not supported by commercial strategies that result in massive audience response.

It must be wonderful to feel that the world is out there for you to see it. The combination between the immensity of the world and the ironies of life will no doubt inspire Kim to explore infinite possibilities. I would add that there are no obstacles ahead, for "he does not seek anything but instead experiences it all for what it is," as Herman Hesse wrote in *Siddhartha*. The name of the book was the name of the Buddha before he renounced his princely fate, and it means "one who has found meaning" of existence. This is Kim's quest, and he seems to be moving in the right direction.

Finally, I asked him a trite question that present biographers of the famous dead can avoid. But Kim, to the good fortune of his audience (for he does have a wide audience, even if he may not think so), is very much alive. Many of those who are eagerly expecting his next films entertain the dream of becoming directors, so I felt bound to speak for them and ask on their behalf what advice he would give them.

More than savvy skills and techniques, I ponder what if [people] observe more carefully and closely the people and phenomena around them.

Filmography and Awards

Crocodile (1996)

Wild Animals (1997)

Birdcage Inn (1998)

The Isle (2000),

Venice International Film Festival, NETPAC
  Special Mention, 2000.
Brussels International Festival of Fantasy Film,
  Golden Crow for Best Film, 2001.
Oporto International Film Festival (Portugal),
  Special Jury Award and Best Actress, 2001.
International Film Festival of Moscow, Special
  Jury Prize, 2001.

Real Fiction (2000)

Address Unknown (2001),

Cinema Novo Film Festival (Belgium),
  Amakourou Prize from young jury, 2002.

Bad Guy (2002),

Fukuaka Asian Film Festival (Japan), Grand
    Prix, 2002.
Grand Bell Awards (Korea), Best Actress to Seo
    Won, 2002.

The Coastguard (2002),

Karlovy Vary International Film Festival
    (Czchech Republic), FIPRESCI Award,
    NETPAC Award for Asian Cinema, Prize of
    the Town Karlovy Vary, 2003.

Spring, Summer, Autumn, Winter . . . and Spring
                    (2003),

Vladivostok International Film Festival, Grand
    Prix for Best Feature, 2004.
Romanian Film Festival Anonimul, Best
    Cinematography, 2004.
Las Palmas International Film Festival
    (Canary Islands, Spain), The Golden Lady
    Harimaguada Award for Best Film; Best
    Cinematography Award, 2004.
Academy Awards, Korea's Official Selection for
    Best Foreign Language Film, 2004.
San Sebastian International Film Festival
    (Spain), Audience Award, 2003.

Locarno International Film Festival
(Switzerland), Junior Jury Award, CICAE/
ARTE prize, NETPAC Award for Asian
Cinema, Don Quijote Award, 2003.

Samaritan Girl (2004)

3-Iron (2004),

Tallinn Black Nights Film Festival (Estonia),
Best Director, Audience Award, Postimees
Jury Prize, Estonian Film Critics Award,
2004.
Valladolid International Film Festival (Spain),
Golden Spike for Best Film, 2004.
Venice International Film Festival, Silver
Lion for Best Director, FIPRESCI Award,
Leoncino d'Oro (Agiscuola), 2004.

The Bow (2005)

Time (2006)

Breath (2007)

Dream (2008)

Film Stills

Crocodile (1996)

Crocodile (1996)

Bad Guy (2002)

Spring, Summer, Autumn, Winter . . . and Spring (2003)

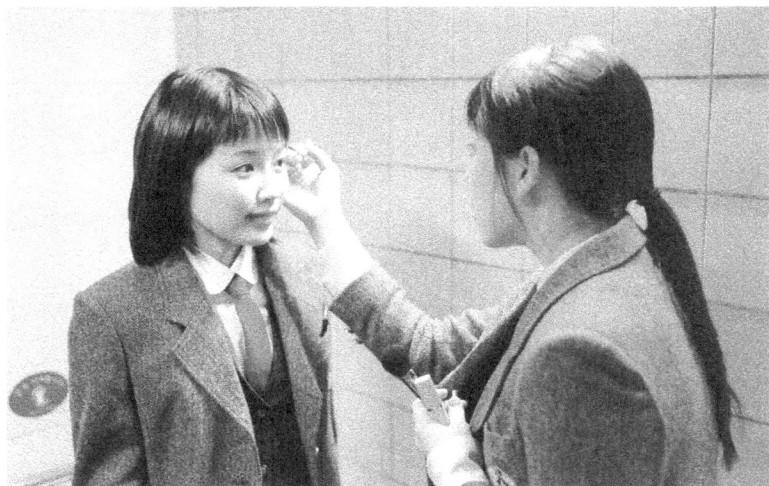

Samaritan Girl (2004)

3-Iron (2004)

3-Iron (2004)

The Bow (2005)

Time (2006)

Breath (2007)

Dream (2008)